LITTLE QUICK FIX:

CHOOSE YOUR STATISTICAL TEST

#LittleQuickFix

LITTLE QUICK FIX:

CHOOSE YOUR STATISTICAL TEST

Maureen Haaker

SAGE

Los Angeles | London | New Delhi
Singapore | Washington DC | Melbourne

SAGE

Los Angeles | London | New Delhi
Singapore | Washington DC | Melbourne

Sage Publications Ltd
1 Oliver's Yard
55 City Road
London EC1Y 1SP

Sage Publications Inc.
2455 Teller Road
Thousand Oaks, California 91320

Sage Publications India Pvt Ltd
B 1/I 1 Mohan Cooperative Industrial Area
Mathura Road
New Delhi 110 044

Sage Publications Asia-Pacific Pte Ltd
3 Church street
#10-04 Samsung hub
Singapore 049483

First published 2019

Editor: Alysha Owen
Editorial assistant: Lauren Jacobs
Production editor: Imogen Roome
Marketing manager: Ben Griffin-Sherwood
Design: Lisa Harper-Wells
Typeset by: C&M Digitals (P) Ltd, Chennai, India
Printed in the UK

Library of Congress Control Number: 2019946176

British Library Cataloguing in Publication data

A catalogue record for this book is available from the British Library.

ISBN 978-1-5264-9252-4

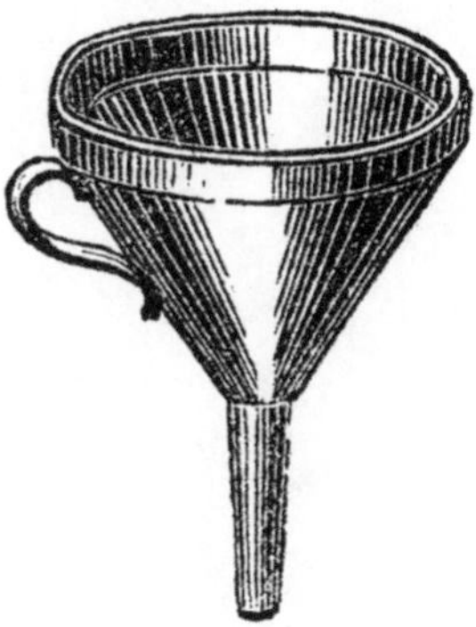

Contents

2 MIN summary

Everything in this book!

Section 1 Descriptive statistics summarize your data and should be reported in every statistical analysis. Measure frequency, central tendency, and dispersion with descriptive statistics.

Section 2 Three easy questions will help you identify your level of measurement and tell you whether your variable categorizes, ranks, or scales your data. Make sure your conclusions about your data are correct.

Section 3 You can compare groups or draw associations or correlations between variables with inferential statistics. Inferential statistics help you generalize from your sample to the wider population.

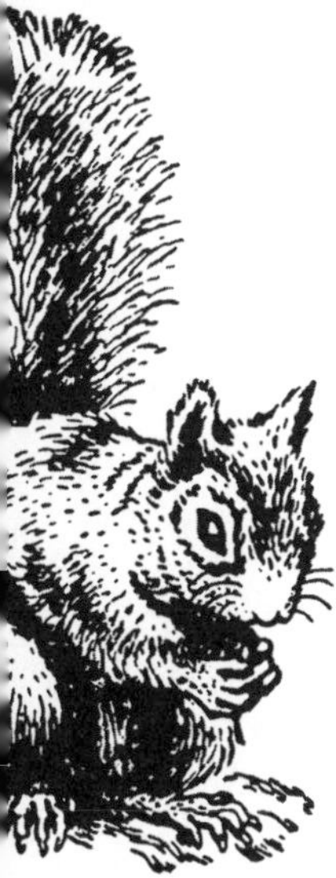

Section 4 Paired groups share a common characteristic that allows you to match up participants or scores in different groups. Independent groups, on the other hand, just group your data and you cannot match scores from different groups.

Section 5 Normal distribution is a spread of scores that graphs into a symmetrical, bell-shaped curve. Most data is assumed to be normally distributed, but watch out for data with outliers, skew or kurtosis, or ordinal level data, which break this assumption and require a different kind of statistical test.

Section 6 Walk through this step-by-step process to evaluate variables and data and decide on the most appropriate statistical test to run.

Section

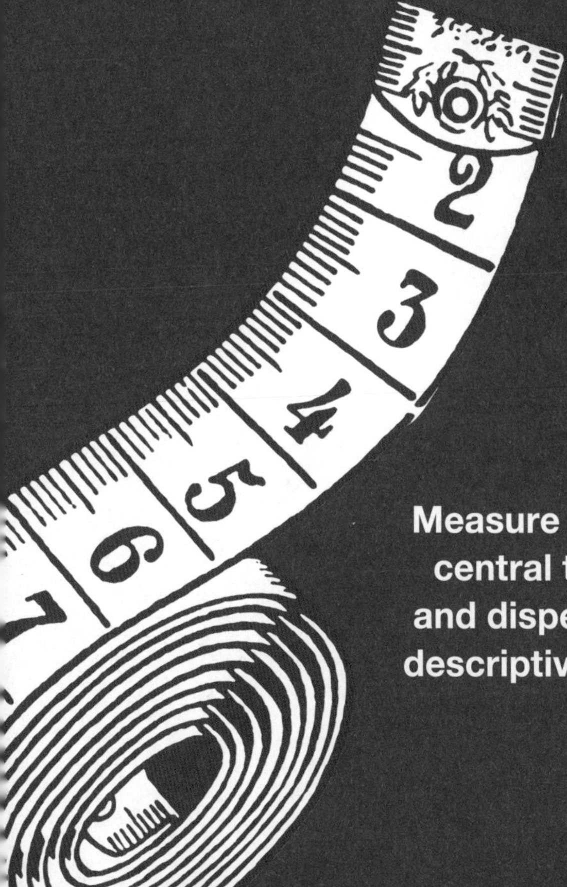

Measure frequency, central tendency, and dispersion with descriptive statistics

Q

What kind of analysis can I run with descriptive statistics?

A

10 SEC summary

Descriptive statistics to help you summarize your data and find unusual patterns, which can be helpful in every statistical analysis.

Write a short summary

You should always consider running some descriptive statistics initially to explore your dataset. Together with some graphical representations, they form the basis of virtually every statistical analysis. Descriptive statistics give a 'glimpse' of your data and help to summarize the key features of the data. There are three main types of descriptive statistics:

- Measures of frequency
- Measures of central tendency
- Measures of dispersion

Ideally, you want to report a mix of these tests in every statistical analysis.

KEEPING IT SHORT AND SWEET

Descriptive statistics will help **reduce your dataset** into a few, easily reportable numbers. As you calculate descriptive statistics, you begin to build up a clear picture about the patterns in your data, and you might be able to determine if there are any data points that lie very far from the mean (also called outliers) or gaps in your dataset. Descriptive statistics is a type of quantitative analysis that allows you to **describe data in a meaningful way**. They allow you to present and visualize raw data, and, therefore inform your understanding of the data so that you are no longer just staring at a number among many other numbers – you can see one number, summarising the whole dataset.

MEASURES OF FREQUENCY

One of the most basic ways to summarise your dataset is to simply count up how many times a particular event or condition occurs within your dataset. This gives a clear idea of the proportions within your dataset. Three common measures of frequency are:

Frequency

Frequency is simply the number of times a data point occurs within a dataset. This will require you to count how many times you see the same value with your dataset – easy!

Distribution curves

Distribution curves plot the frequency of each data point onto a graph, then draw a 'line of best fit' which connects all (or at least most!) of these points.

Per cent

Per cent literally means 'per 100'. As a measure of frequency, percentages will tell you how often the data point will come up every 100 occurrences. To find out a percentage, take the frequency, divide it by the total number of data points and multiply by 100.

MEASURES OF CENTRAL TENDENCY

One of the key assumptions of quantitative data is that data will cluster around a central value. This 'measure of central tendency' is **one of the commonly reported descriptive statistics**. The three measures of central tendency are:

Mean

Commonly known as the average, the mean is probably the most used measure of central tendency. It adds up all data points together and divides that sum by the number of data points.

Median

If you line up all the values in your dataset in increasing order, the median will be the number right in the middle. Medians should be used instead of the mean if you have extreme values, or outliers, in your data.

Mode

The mode is the data point that is recorded most frequently. It's not used often but it is also helpful if you have a lot of outliers.

MEASURES OF DISPERSION

No matter what you are measuring, there will always be some level of variation – it is nearly impossible for all data points to be the exact same! Measures of dispersion will tell you the extent to which values can vary within your sample.

Range

Range is the simplest measure of dispersion and is reported as either a number (e.g. 'The range was 54.') or a set of the minimum and maximum numbers (e.g. 'The range was 26 to 80.').

Standard deviation

Standard deviation gives you a good idea about how tightly clustered data points are around the central tendency. It's also standardized, meaning that it gives a very consistent measure of how far away points are from each other.

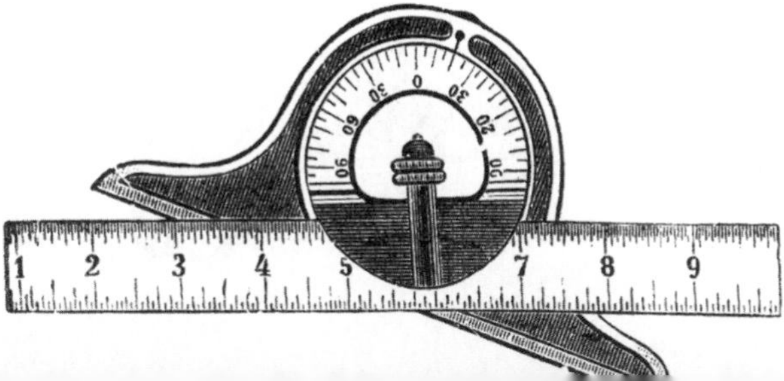

MAKING THE MOST OF YOUR DATA

Do not make the mistake of drawing conclusions beyond what your analyses can provide: **descriptive statistics do not allow you to make generalisations** about patterns in the wider population. Rather, descriptive statistics only describe the data sample. When you see, for example, an average reported, this can only speak to the sample from which the average was calculated – you should not claim that the average is the same for *everyone*.

This is a common mistake, and you can probably find lots of examples in the news of where an average is implied to be the same for everyone! Although you can't generalize with descriptive statistics, they can still **help you understand patterns in your dataset and present large amounts of data in a meaningful way.**

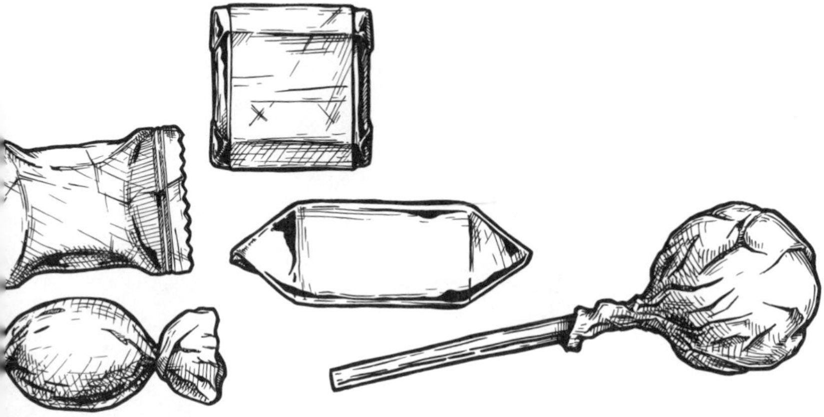

REPORTING MEASURES OF FREQUENCY

Let's work with the following dataset to calculate measures of frequency. The following set of numbers reports the shoe size of a football team:

{6, 8, 10, 8, 7, 10, 9, 8, 7, 9, 12, 9, 10, 11, 9}

Frequency and percentages

To report frequencies, we just need to say how many players there are with each shoe size and the total number of players in our dataset. To calculate percentages, you'll need to divide the frequency by the total number of players, then multiply by 100.

Finish the following table to report the frequency and percentage of each shoe size.

Shoe Size	Frequency (in number of players)	Percentage
6	1	6.7%
7		13.3%
8	3	
9		
10	3	20%
11		6.7%
12	1	
Total	15	100%

See answers on P22

Distribution curve

This graph plots the shoe size along the x-axis (at the bottom) and frequencies on the y-axis (along the left-hand side).

Draw a curved to line to connect the dots:

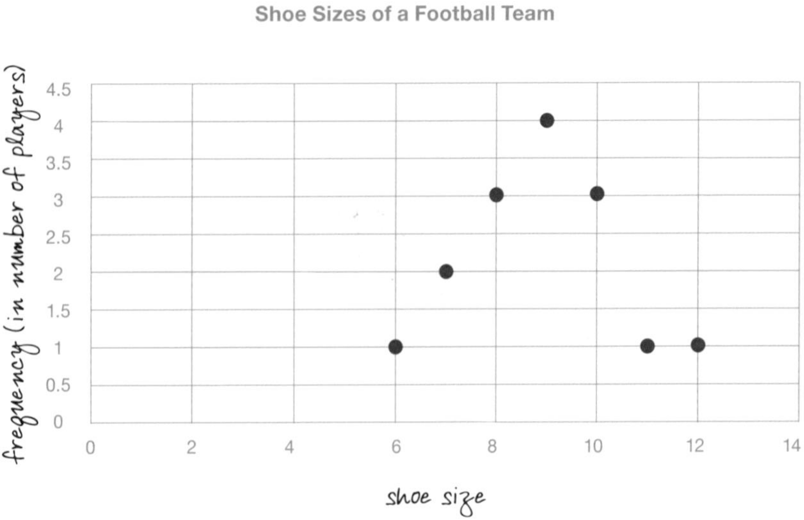

REPORTING MEASURES OF CENTRAL TENDENCY AND DISPERSION

DO IT YOURSEL

Let's work with the same dataset of shoe sizes of a football team, but now calculate the measures of central tendency and dispersion.

Mean, median and mode

Complete the following equation to find the **mean**:

$$\frac{(6 + 8 + 10 + 8 + 7 + 10 + 9 + 8 + 7 + 9 + 12 + 9 + 10 + 11 + 9)}{15} =$$

For the **median**, you need to line up all data points in increasing size. Fill in the rest of the line, then circle the number in the middle:

{6, ___, ___, ___, ___, ___, ___, ___, ___, ___, ___, ___, ___, ___, ___, 12}

To find the **mode**, revisit the frequency table you filled in on the previous page. Which shoe size does the greatest number of players have? In other words, which shoe size has the highest frequency?

Range

Report back the minimum and maximum shoe size within this dataset.

The range of shoe sizes is ___ to ___.

See answers on P23

ANSWERS

Check your answers

Shoe Size	Frequency (in number of players)	Percentage
6	1	6.7%
7	2	13.3%
8	3	20%
9	4	26.7%
10	3	20%
11	1	6.7%
12	1	6.7%
Total	15	100%

DO IT YOURSELF

ANSWERS

Check your answers

Mean

$$\frac{(6 + 8 + 10 + 8 + 7 + 10 + 9 + 8 + 7 + 9 + 12 + 9 + 10 + 11 + 9)}{15}$$

$= (\frac{133}{15} = 9\ (8.9))$

Median

{6, 7, 7, 8, 8, 8, 9, (9), 9, 9, 10, 10, 10, 11, 12}

Mode

9

Range

The range of shoe sizes is 6 to 12.

CHECKPOINT

TEST YOUR KNOWLEDGE

Answer the questions below.

What do descriptive statistics do?

....

....

What are three measures used in descriptive statistics?

....

....

What can't you do with descriptive statistics?

....

....

When should you report descriptive statistics?

....

....

CHECKPOINT

ANSWERS

What do descriptive statistics do?

Summarize your data

What are three measures used in descriptive statistics?

Frequency, central tendency, and dispersion

What can't you do with descriptive statistics?

Generalize

When should you report descriptive statistics?

With every statistical analysis

2 Section

Make sure
your conclusions
about your data
are correct

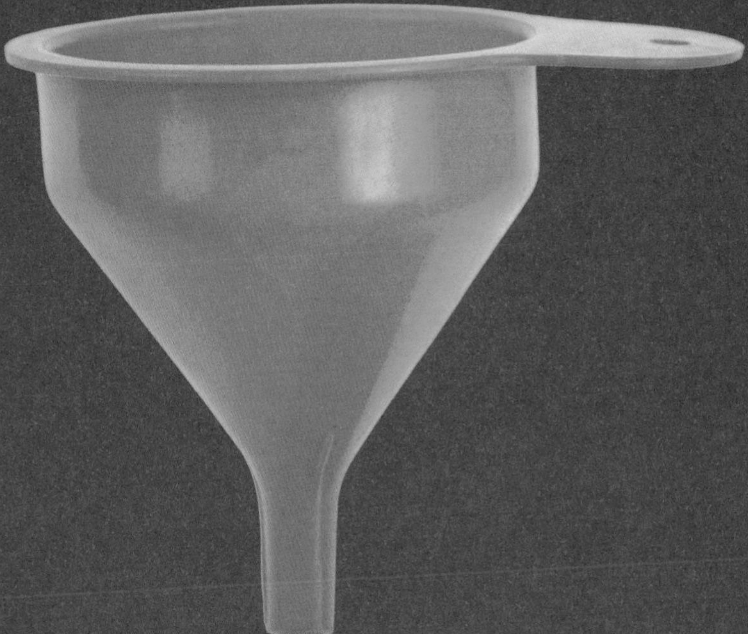

Q

How do I identify the level of measurement?

A

summary

The level of measurement will indicate if the variable you are studying is measured by difference (categories), the direction of difference (ranks), or the amount of difference (scales).

Get organized

Levels of measurements look closely at how you defined, or operationalized, your variables, so you'll need to look at how the data is recorded to determine a level of measurement. There are four levels of measurement:

- Nominal
- Ordinal
- Interval
- Ratio

Nominal and ordinal data are categorical and mean that your data is grouped into distinct groups. Interval and ratio data are scaled, which means they are measured using numbers. Knowing what level of measurement your data is will help you assess and organize your variables and decide which statistical test to run.

NOMINAL

Nominal level of measurement is the most basic way to define and measure data. This is where data is grouped into discrete categories. **Discrete categories** mean there is no overlap between groups – data clearly fall into one category and one category only.

Categories should be exhaustive – all data should be able to be put into a group. A common example of nominal data is sex. When you record the sex of people, you are categorising them into groups of male or female. Other examples of nominal data include:

- Religion (e.g. Christian, Muslim, Jewish, etc.)
- Political affiliation (e.g. Conservative, Liberal, Centre, etc.)
- Hair colour (e.g. blonde, brown, black, or other)
- Type of accommodation (e.g. house, apartment, trailer, or other)

ORDINAL

This is categorical data (just like nominal data) which **can be ranked**. Rankings mean that data is placed on a scale where one category can be 'more' or 'better' than another category.

This is not a standardized scale. For example, placement in a spelling bee (e.g. 1st, 2nd, 3rd, etc.) is ordinal data – you can score higher by placing higher in the spelling bee, but you may not know how much better you have to do in order to place higher. Other examples of ordinal data include:

- Likert-type scale (strongly agree, agree, disagree, strongly disagree)
- Level of education (e.g. BA or BSc, MA or MSc, PhD)
- A hot pepper scale (measuring spiciness – e.g. hot, hotter, hottest)
- Socioeconomic class (e.g. poor, middle class, rich)

INTERVAL

Unlike nominal and ordinal data, interval data is continuous. This is where data is numerical *(rather than categorical) and falls onto a scale.* **Every point on the scale should be an equal distance from one another.**

The scales used to measure interval data, however, **have an arbitrary zero point**. A common example of interval data is temperature. Temperature is on a scale of Celsius or Fahrenheit, however '0 degrees' doesn't mean there is no temperature – it's just a random point on the scale called zero. Other examples of interval data include:

- IQ score
- GPS coordinates (measured in latitudinal or longitudinal degrees)
- Quantitative rating scales (such as the Quality of Life (CASP-19) scale)
- Time on a clock

RATIO

Ratio data is the highest level of measurement. Like interval data, ratio data is quantitative, continuous, and falls onto a scale. Unlike interval data, however, **ratio data has an absolute zero**. In other words, a zero on this scale is meaningful – it's something everyone knows and understands.

An example of ratio data is time (measured in seconds). All points on this 'scale' have an equal amount of difference, and everyone understands what zero seconds means. Other examples of ratio data include:

- Amount of money
- Number of children
- *Standardized* scales (such as the PHQ-9 scale for depression)
- Number of days spent in jail

ANOTHER WAY TO THINK ABOUT THE LEVELS OF MEASUREMENT

	Nominal	Ordinal	Interval	Ratio
Indicates Difference	✓	✓	✓	✓
Indicates Difference and Direction		✓	✓	✓
Indicates Amount of Difference			✓	✓
Has Absolute Zero				✓

To figure out the level of measurement, ask yourself these three questions about your data:

Is there an intrinsic ranking (is one outcome 'better' or 'more' than another)?

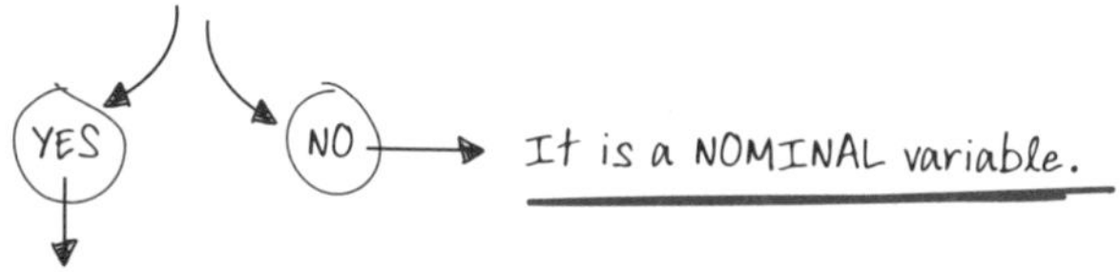

Is there a measurable difference between rankings (is the difference between every ranking the same)?

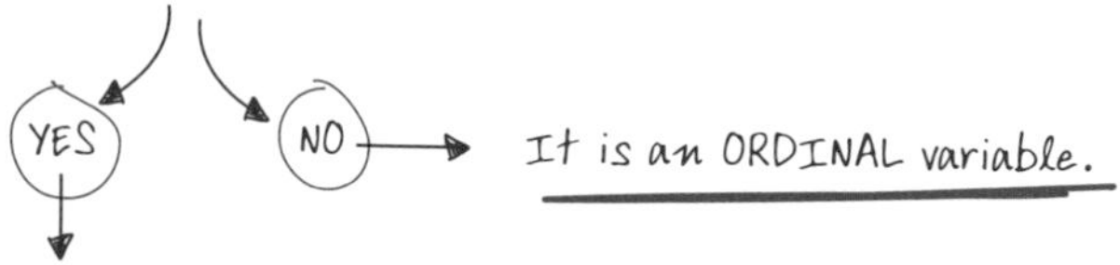

Is there an absolute zero (as opposed to an arbitrary zero)?

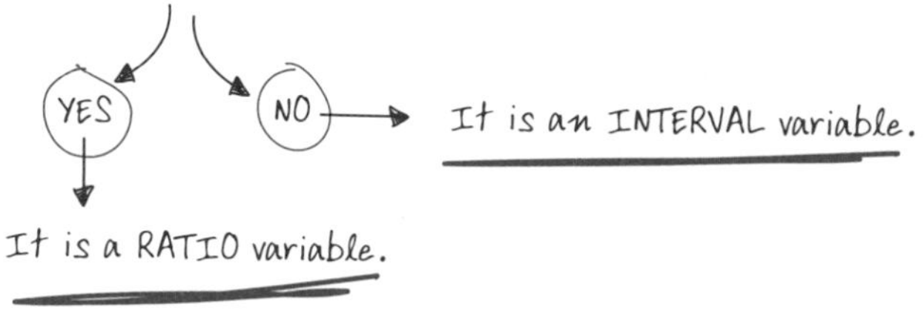

WHY DOES THE LEVEL OF MEASUREMENT MATTER?

You are unlikely to report levels of measurement in your results. These classifications, however, **remind us to not to make inappropriate claims about the data**. For example, let's say two stores (store A and store B) use a rating scale to find out their customer satisfaction. Store A averages 6.0 and store B averages 3.0. We need to be careful not to assert that satisfaction is twice as high in store A as store B. Although a difference exists, we cannot make a proportional claim about the data since customer satisfaction scales are interval level data and do not have an absolute zero. Therefore, we cannot say for certain that satisfaction is 'double'. Sometimes you can change the level the level of measurement to suit the claim you want to make – you just need to change the way you ask the question.

DO IT YOURSELF

'BIN' YOUR VARIABLE INTO A DIFFERENT LEVEL OF MEASUREMENT

You can change the level of measurement of a variable by changing the way the question is asked. Let's take a look at age for example.

You could ask a ratio-level question, where the answers to a survey question on age would have an absolute zero. How might you phrase this question?

Answer: What is your age?

Now we want to ask this question at the ordinal-level. Age naturally has a ranking (one outcome is 'older' than another), which makes this a little easier. However, ordinal-level data does not have the same 'distance' between each category of age, like in this example:

What is your age?

- ☐ Under 18
- ☐ 19–29
- ☐ 30–39
- ☐ 40 and over

Write your own categories of age, making sure that the number of years in each category is not equal.

Finally, you can even ask about age in a way that could make nominal-level data:

What is your age?

- ☐ Child
- ☐ Adolescent
- ☐ Adult

The rank on this question is weak, and the boundaries between each category are fuzzy – one 18-year-old may mark 'adolescent' while another may mark 'adult'.

This process of moving between levels of measurement is also called 'binning' variables.

CHECKPOINT

YOUR TURN!

Use the flow chart on page 37, to identify the level of measurement for the following variables:

1. Temperature (measured in degrees Celsius)
2. Gender
3. Time (measured in seconds)
4. Political orientation (e.g. conservative, centre, liberal)
5. Race/ethnicity
6. Customer satisfaction (e.g. very satisfied, satisfied, not satisfied)
7. Grade (measured in a score out of 100)
8. Number of days spent at sea
9. Degrees north of the equator
10. Standardized scale measuring depression

ANSWERS

1 Interval

2 Nominal

3 Ratio

4 Nominal

5 Nominal

6 Ordinal

7 Ratio

8 Ratio

9 Interval

10 Ratio

CHECKPOINT

Congratulations!

On a scale of 1–10, my confidence for determining levels of measurementis now ____.

#LittleQuickFix

Section 3

Inferential statistics help you generalize from your sample to the wider population

Q

What kind of analysis can I run with inferential statistics?

A

10 SEC

summary

Inferential statistics can be used to generalize findings to larger populations. In other words, they help you make accurate inferences from a sample.

Go further with inferential statistics

Inferential statistics help you make generalisations (and future predictions!) about data. When calculating inferential statistics, it is crucial that the sample is representative of the entire population. There are two key goals of inferential statistics:

- To establish an association, or relationship, between two variables
- To make a comparison between two variables

The point you want to make with your data will help you determine which inferential test you should run.

One of the first steps of quantitative research is to define, recruit or collect a sample. It would be impossible to collect data from every single person or source that the research question is asking about, so sampling makes research feasible. If you've collected a **representative sample**, then you can confidently draw conclusions which extend beyond your data to the wider population. For example, we might infer from our data what the whole population might think. Or we might compare groups and decide if differences were just happenchance of the study or if those groups actually have a real difference. If your sample is not representative, you may be committing a sampling error, which will mean you shouldn't generalize to the wider population. But with a representative sample, you can start to make inferences.

TO MAKE – OR NOT TO MAKE – GENERALISATIONS

There are a couple of different kinds of connections you might want to establish when using inferential statistics:

- Associations
- Comparisons

In order to know which one to use, you need to think about what conclusion you want to make. Do you want to show a relationship between variables or compare groups? Showing relationships would need to be done using a test that measures associations. Comparing groups, however, would require a different sort of test that can specifically make comparisons.

WHAT IS YOUR GOAL?

Association is just another word for **describing a relationship, or correlation, between variables.** Some statistical tests which test associations can also – on top of just telling you there is an association – **measure the strength and direction of the relationship.**

For example, if you were looking at student attendance and exam grades, you might find a correlation which shows that the more students attend class, the higher their grades are. But your statistical test would also be able to tell how strongly correlated these two events are. Correlation coefficients are a measure of the strength of the association between two variables. It does not, however, distinguish between independent and dependent variables, nor does it determine a cause-and-effect relationship. So remember the old saying: correlation does not mean causation!

ASSOCIATION

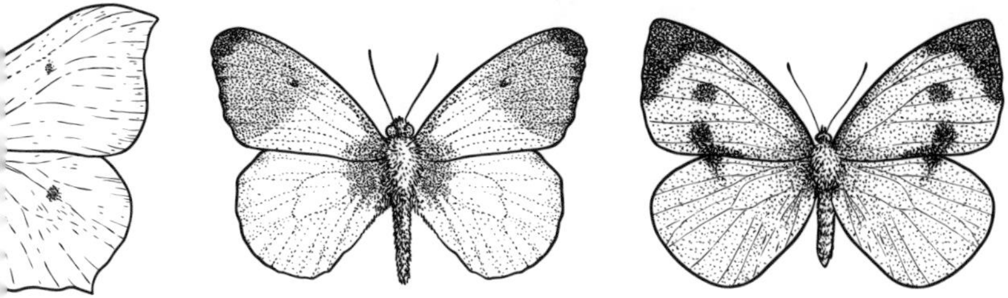

Common statistical tests which establish an association are:

- Chi Square*
- Pearson's correlation coefficient
- Spearman's correlation coefficient

* It's worth pointing out that while correlation coefficients can tell you the exact strength of the relationship between variables, Chi-Square test cannot - it will only tell you if the relationship is significant.

STATISTICAL TESTS FOR ASSOCIATIONS

Comparisons look at the differences between groups in your data. For example, you might be interested to see if there is a significant different between genders and their performance on IQ tests, or you might want to see if different age groups have different reflex times. You could just see what the average, or mean, is for each group and see how large a difference there is between means. However, inferential statistics which measure comparisons go one step further and look at the difference between means and variability. Inferential statistics which compare will be able to **check the difference between means and variability** to see just how similar or different groups really are from each other.

COMPARISON

Variability tells you how wide a distribution curve is. A high variability in groups means there is a good chance of overlap in the distribution curves, while a low variability means there could be very little overlap. Look at these images. Which of the following graphs do you think has the most difference?

(Hint: Notice how the means (drawn with blue dotted lines) look to be about the same? Look instead at how much the distribution curves overlap.)

Low variability

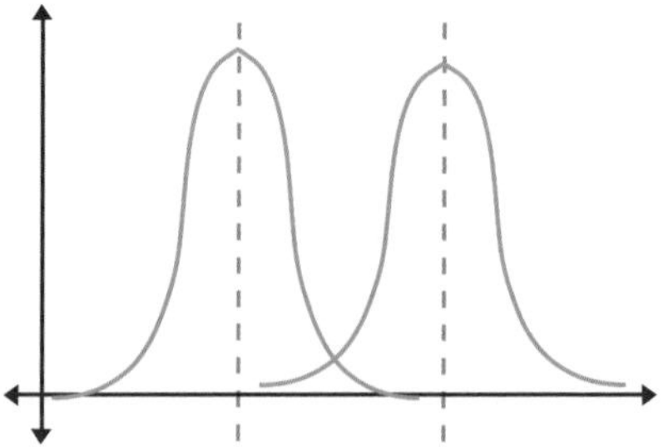

Medium variability

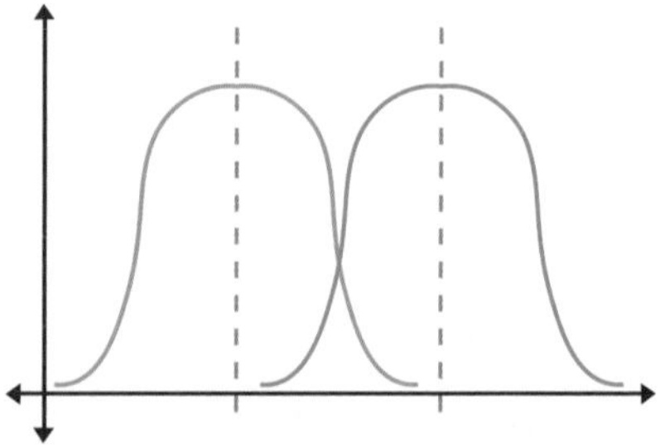

High variability

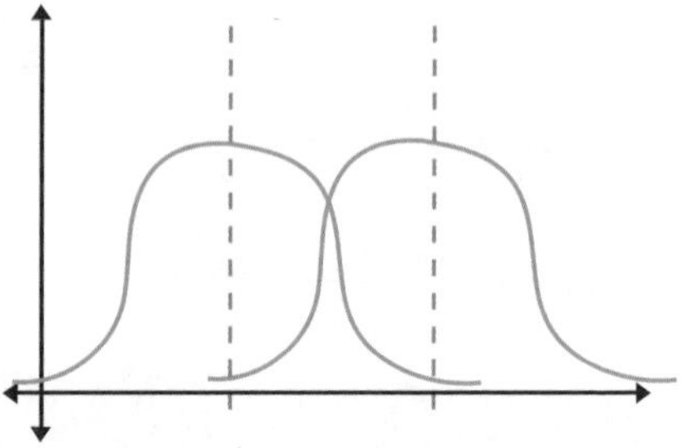

They all have the same difference between their means, so the variability determines how different the groups are. Since the first graph (with low variability) shows the least overlap, this is the one showing the most difference between groups.

Common statistical tests which allow you to compare are:

- Independent t-test
- Paired t-test
- One-way, repeated measures ANOVA
- One-way, independent measures ANOVA
- Kruskal-Wallis test
- Friedman's test
- 1-sample Wilcoxon
- Mann-Whitney test

STATISTICAL TESTS FOR COMPARISONS

When deciding on the most appropriate inferential statistic, you may find yourself looking at two variables trying to figure out what connection you are trying to make. If you can't decide on whether you are making an association, correlation, or comparison, then **your levels of measurement can help you out**. Inferential statistics generally follow these rules:

If you have...	**...then you should...**
2 nominal or ordinal level variables	draw an association with Chi-Square
2 interval or ratio level variables	make a correlation with Pearson's or Spearman's correlation coefficient
1 nominal or ordinal level variable and 1 interval or ratio level variable	make a comparison using a t-test, ANOVA, or equivalent.

This is not a complete rule of thumb – Section 5 will give you some options outside of this, but this is a way to use your levels of measurement to signpost you to the right batch of statistics you can run on the data.

MAKE THE CONNECTION

In general, all inferential statistics, whether tested with a representative population or not, come with (even a very small!) level of uncertainty. With inferential statistics, you are providing information about a population that you have not fully measured, and consequently it is important to remember that inferential statistics are conclusions that *support* your conclusions – they never *prove* your conclusions.

MAKING THE MOST OF YOUR DATA

CHECKPOINT

Get it?

Q: What are two types of inferences that can you draw using inferential statistics?

Got it!

A: Associations and comparisons

Congratulations!

I know what I want to find out - now it's time to assess my variables and data.

#LittleQuickFix

Paired groups share a common characteristic. On the other hand, independent groups just group your data

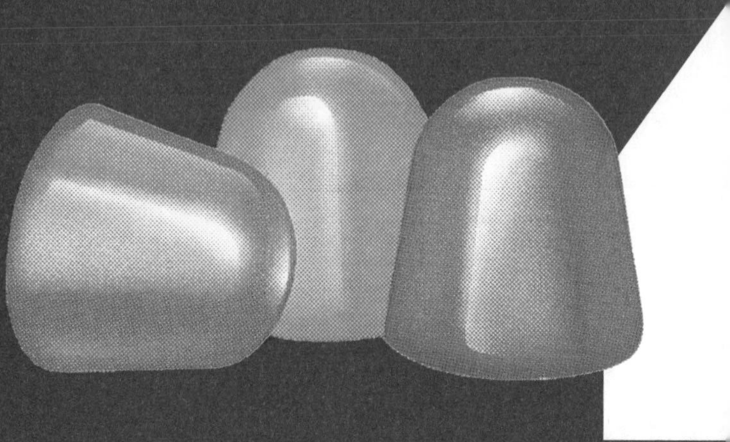

Section 4

Q

What is the difference between paired and independent groups?

A

10 SEC summary

Independent groups are where data has been randomly selected, while paired groups mean data points can be matched to a data point in another group.

Know your groups

When you want to make a comparison, you need decide what groups you are going to compare. There are two key considerations which will help you determine which (of the many!) statistical tests to run that will allow you to compare groups:

1. **How many groups** are you comparing? (Two? Three or more?)
2. Are the groups **paired or independent?**

Paired groups share some kind of link – whether it is the same participant who is assessed several times, or there is something about the people in each group that share something in common. Independent groups, on the other hand, don't share any characteristics; they are random groupings which cannot be cannot be connected in any way.

GO COMPARE

If you've decided you want to run a statistical test that will give you a comparison, you have a few different things to think about to really nail down what you are comparing.

- First, you need to **think about what variable, or characteristic, you are comparing.** Perhaps you want to compare genders, age groups, or social classes. No matter what distinguishes your groups, it will require you to compare based on data that is nominal or ordinal level, since you will need categories to group data into.

- Next, you need to decide **how many groups** you are comparing. While some are instinctive (e.g. comparing genders usually means comparing two groups), you may need to decide how you are dividing up the data for other characteristics (such as social class, which can be divided up a number of ways).

- Finally, you need to decide **if the groups are paired or independent.** There's more on that later in this section.

IT'S ALL ABOUT THE NUMBERS

Sometimes when analysing data, you may want to compare results across different subsets, or groups, of data. You may already have a variable that naturally divides your data up into groups because it is categorical (so it's nominal or ordinal data). Alternatively, you might have created groups in the data by 'binning' the variable (remember from Section 2 – 'binning' variables requires you to artificially create groups and lower the level of measurement). Once you've determined your groups, the number of groups can help determine what test you can run.

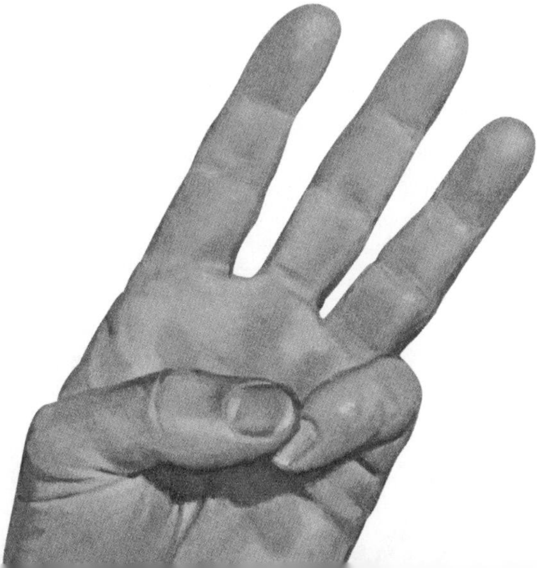

You might not want to split up the data, so you only have one big group of data. Conversely, you might want to compare two groups (such as males versus females). Or, you might want to compare three or more groups (such as comparing scores across different regions or between groups of people based on their native language). If you have divided your data up into groups, you'll need to think about how many groups you are comparing – **comparing two groups will require different kinds of statistical tests than when you are comparing three or more groups.**

PAIRED GROUPS

Paired groups, also sometimes called dependent groups, are based on **groups which are related to each other**. This is where a data point, or score, in one group can be easily coupled to a data point, or score, in another group. Where groups are paired, it simply means that the groups are somehow linked to each other.

Examples of paired groups include:

- Pre-test/post-test scores (where something is measured before and after an intervention)
- Matched samples (where individuals are matched with someone who shares all the same characteristics except the one under investigation)
- Duplicate measures (where you might be measuring the same thing several times over a period of time)
- Cross-over trials (where the same individual might be put in different environments or given alternative treatments)

INDEPENDENT GROUPS

Independent groups, sometimes also called unrelated groups, are basically the opposite of paired groups. This is where there is no logical way to match data points across different groups. Independent groups are **unrelated by design**, so the data in one group does not depend upon the values of any other group. Unlike paired groups, we wouldn't normally expect there to be a huge difference (unless, of course, you have a significant finding!).

Independent groups are common – any time you want to compare groups (for example, males versus females; outcomes in different regions; those who exercise versus those who don't, etc.), it's often independent groups.

WHAT TEST DO I RUN?

Use this handy table to select the best test to use.

Grouping	Statistical test
Comparing one group to a hypothetical, or ideal, value that you might normally expect to see based on your calculations	Chi-square Wilcoxon test One-samples t-test
Comparing two independent groups	Independent t-test Mann-Whitney test Fisher's test
Comparing two paired groups	Paired t-test Wilcoxon test McNemar's test
Comparing three or more independent groups	One-way ANOVA Kruskal-Wallis test Chi-square
Comparing three or more dependent groups	Repeated-measures ANOVA Friedman test

CHECKPOINT

PAIRED AND INDEPENDENT GROUPS

Below is a quick description of research projects that are aiming to compare two or more groups. Decide if these groups are paired or independent.

1 **A research project is comparing the education outcomes of twins. Group 1 is the twin that was born first, and group 2 is the twin that was born second.**

....

2 **A research project is comparing the running times of male and female runners. Group 1 is males and group 2 is females.**

....

3 **A research project is looking at the effectiveness of a new drug for those with depression. Participants are scored on a standardized depression scale before taking the drug (group 1), one month after starting the drug (group 2), and six months after taking the drug (group 3).**

....

4 **A research project is doing an international study on criminal justice and wants to compare the average jail times across three countries in Europe. Group 1 is in jail times for inmates in the United Kingdom. Group 2 is jail times for inmates from Belgium. Group 3 is jail times for inmates from Italy.**

5 **A research project wants to look at the amount of time that married, heterosexual couples spend on household chores. Group 1 is the women and group 2 is the men.**

Answers

1 Paired 2 Independent 3 Paired 4 Independent 5 Paired

Normal distribution is a spread of scores that graphs into a symmetrical, bell-shaped curve

Section 5

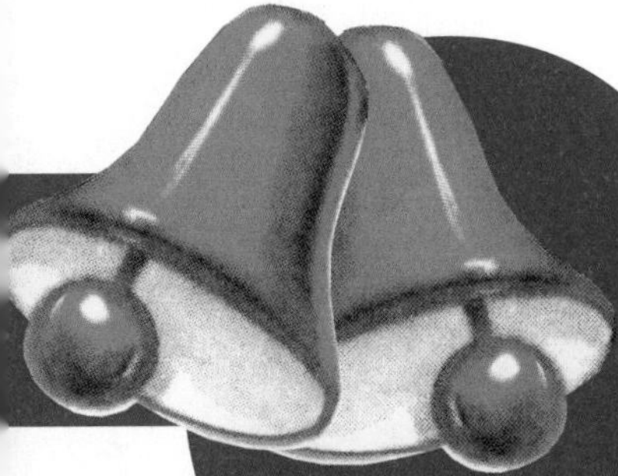

Q

How can I tell if my data is normally distributed?

A

10 SEC
summary

Interval or ratio data follows a normal distribution if there are no extreme values, skew, or kurtosis in the distribution curve.

Map out your data

Normal distributions are a really important shape in statistics and are considered to be the 'natural' distribution shape for everything. **It's a basic assumption we make about how the world works.** When you plot your data on a distribution curve and it makes this perfectly symmetrical, bell-shaped curve, then you are probably working with parametric data. Parametric data means you can run parametric statistics, which tend to be very accurate. Sometimes, however, you are dealing with data that is not normally distributed (or you can't tell if it is normally distributed), so you need to run a non-parametric test. Non-parametric tests are still accurate, but not quite as accurate as parametric tests. Regardless, it's nice to have options whatever your data throws at you!

WHAT IS A NORMAL DISTRIBUTION?

Statistical tests – and probability – usually assume that data fits into a normal distribution. A normal distribution is an extremely important shape: if you plot every data point onto a graph, a normal distribution of your data would be **shaped like a bell and symmetrical.** The image below shows what a normal distribution looks like. Note the nice bell-shaped curve which is symmetrical.

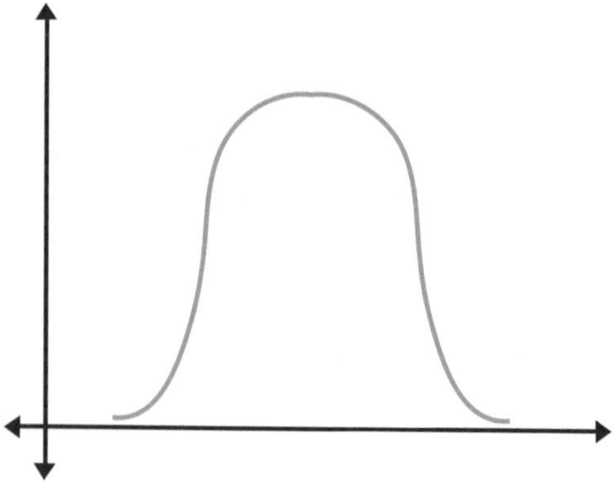

WHAT IF MY DATA ISN'T NORMALLY DISTRIBUTED?

Sometimes, however, data doesn't fit into a normal distribution if it has:

- Skew (the distribution slants to one side)
- Kurtosis (the curve is not a bell-shape – it either comes to a point or is flat on top)
- Extreme values, or outliers
- When data is measured at the ordinal (rather than interval/ratio) level

MAKING ASSUMPTIONS ABOUT DATA

Most statistical tests assume data is normally distributed. This means that a test assumes the **data follows certain rules, or parameters**. When you have normally distributed data, you can run a parametric test. Sometimes, however, you know your data is not normally distributed. Maybe you looked at a distribution and saw the curve wasn't a bell shape, or maybe you spotted some outliers already in your data. Never fear! You still have options – statistical tests have a non-parametric option you can run if you think your data is not normally distributed.

Is the variable you are measuring ordinal level?

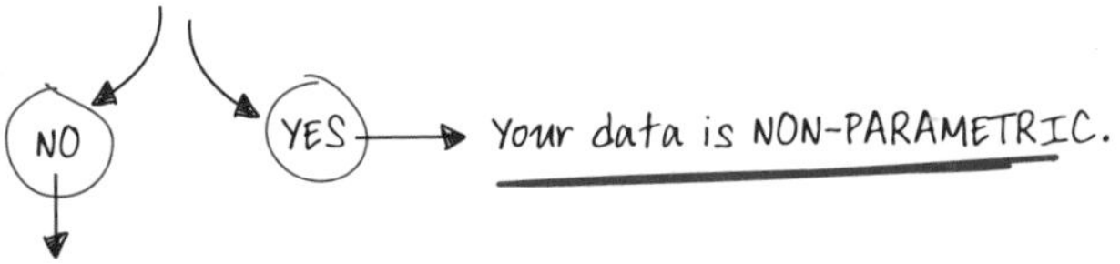

Look closely at the data. Do you see any outliers, or values that are far from the average?

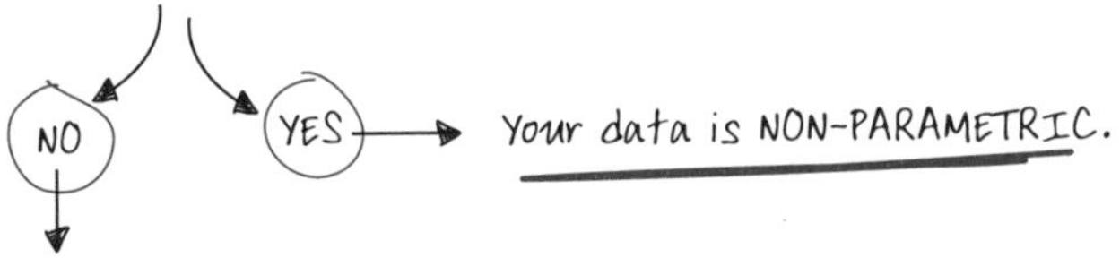

Now look closely at the distribution curve. Do you see a skew (curve leaning to one side) or kurtosis (a curve with a flat or pointy top instead of curve)?

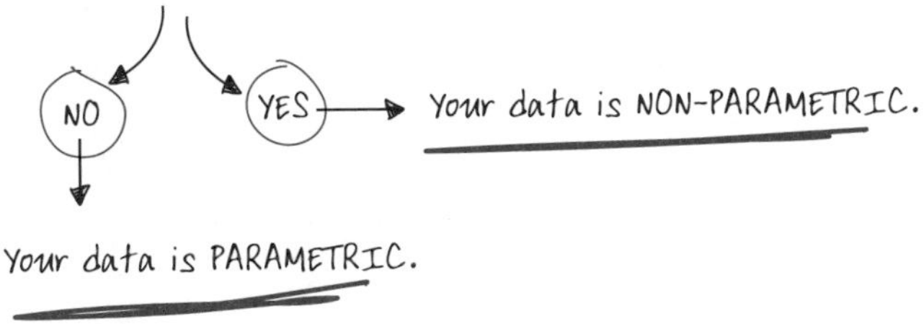

MAKING THE MOST OF YOUR DATA

Nonparametric tests are simpler and less affected by outliers than their parametric counterparts. Technically, you can run a non-parametric test on parametric data too. **Non-parametric tests simply lower the threshold of the parameters that your data has to meet,** so technically it will work on parametric or non-parametric data – even though parametric data is able to meet a higher threshold. However, if you run a non-parametric test on parametric data, you will get a less reliable result with a lower degree of confidence. Non-parametric tests may also require a larger sample to obtain statistically significant findings.

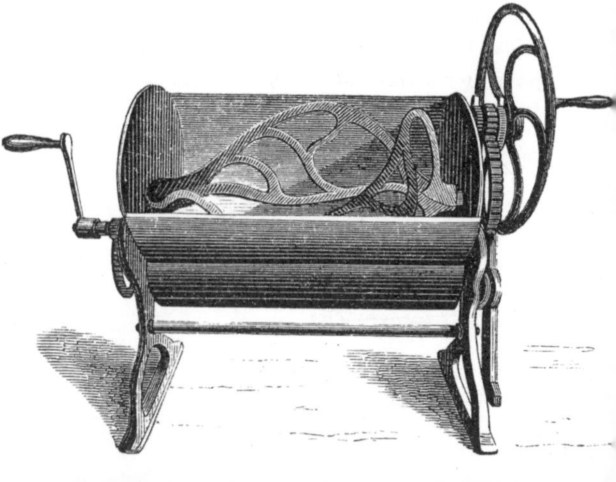

Here's a list of parametric tests and their non-parametric equivalent:

Parametric tests of means	Non-parametric tests of medians
Pearson's correlation	Spearman's Rho
Independent t-test	1-sample Wilcoxon
Paired t-test	Mann-Whitney test
Independent measures ANOVA	Kruskal-Wallis
Repeated measures ANOVA	Friedman's test

WHAT ARE THE REASONS TO RUN NON-PARAMETRIC STATISTIC?

Reason 1: **Your data has a skew or kurtosis.**

A distribution curve allows you to see the shape of your distribution. If it doesn't make the 'ideal' bell-shape, then run a non-parametric test.

Reason 2: **You have extreme values.**

Extreme values, or outliers, affect the validity of parametric tests, so you should run a non-parametric test if you spot any outliers (even if they don't cause a skew in your distribution).

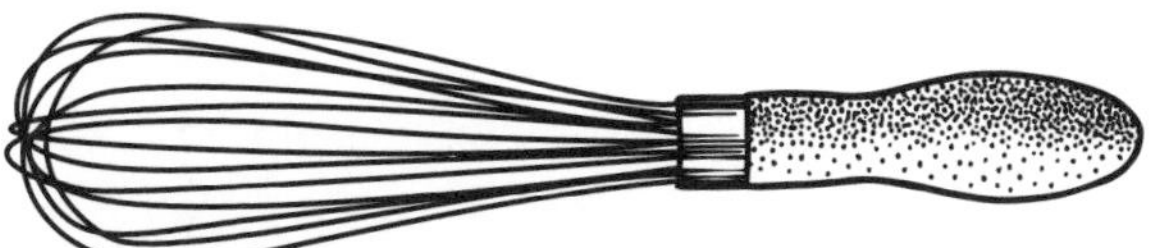

Reason 3: **You have a very small sample size.**

It can be difficult to be confident your data is normally distributed if you don't have enough data to determine this! Run a non-parametric test if you're not sure.

Reason 4: **You have ordinal level data.**

As a general rule, scale and interval data are used in parametric tests, while ordinal data always requires a non-parametric test.

CHECKPOINT

Got it?

Q: What three features in your data give the hint that your data is NOT normally distributed?

Got it!

A: Outliers, skew, or kurtosis

SECTION 6

DIY: DECIDE ON THE MOST APPROPRIATE STATISTICAL TEST TO RUN

HOW TO ASSESS YOUR VARIABLES AND DATA

In this section, you will need to assess the variables and data from a research project to see if you can apply what you've learned. Below is a snippet of the first seven questions in the survey passed out for this piece of research. Answer the questions as they guide you through assessing the variables and data for this research project.

1 What is your age?

....

2 What is your sex?

- ☐ Male
- ☐ Female
- ☐ Other

3 What level of education have you completed?

- ☐ A-levels or equivalent
- ☐ BA/BSc
- ☐ MA/MSc
- ☐ PhD

4 What is your occupation?

....

5 What is your estimated salary per year?

....

6 On the following scale, how satisfied are you with your new product?

- ☐ Very satisfied
- ☐ Satisfied
- ☐ Neither satisfied nor dissatisfied
- ☐ Dissatisfied
- ☐ Very dissatisfied

7 On the following scale, how likely are you to buy another product from us?

- ☐ Very likely
- ☐ Somewhat likely
- ☐ Not at all likely

ASSESS YOUR VARIABLES

1

The levels of measurement for the variables in each of the questions are:

(Tip! go back to the flow chart in section 3 if you are stuck)

1 ....

2 ....

3 ....

4 ....

5 ....

6 ....

7 ....

Answers

1 Ratio 2 Nominal 3 Ordinal 4 Nominal 5 Ratio
6 Ordinal 7 Ordinal

2

DETERMINE YOUR GROUPS

Imagine you want to compare the salaries of respondents by gender. Would these be independent or paired groups?

Independent

Answers

3

ASSESS YOUR DATA

Now let's assess the data. Below are distribution curves of the salaries of men and women.

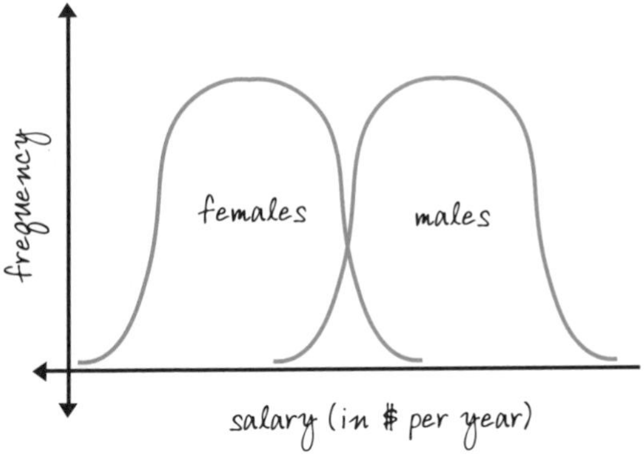

Look closely at the distribution curves:

- Are there any outliers? ☐ Yes ☐ No
- Are either of the distribution curves skewed? ☐ Yes ☐ No
- Do you see any kurtosis in either of the distribution curves? ☐ Yes ☐ No
- Is the data parametric or non-parametric?

(Tip! go back to the flow chart in Section 5 if you are stuck)

....

Answers

1 No 2 No 3 No 4 Parametric

4

PIECE IT ALL TOGETHER AND CHOOSE YOUR STATISTICAL TEST

Now that you've assessed the variables, groups, and data, now you are ready to compare mean salaries by gender. Circle the name of the inferential test that you would use.

(Tip! check the chart of statistical tests in section 5 and the list comparison test in section 2)

Independent t-test

Spearman's correlation coefficient

Repeated measures ANOVA

Mann-Whitney test

Chi Square

Paired t-test

Answers

Independent t-test

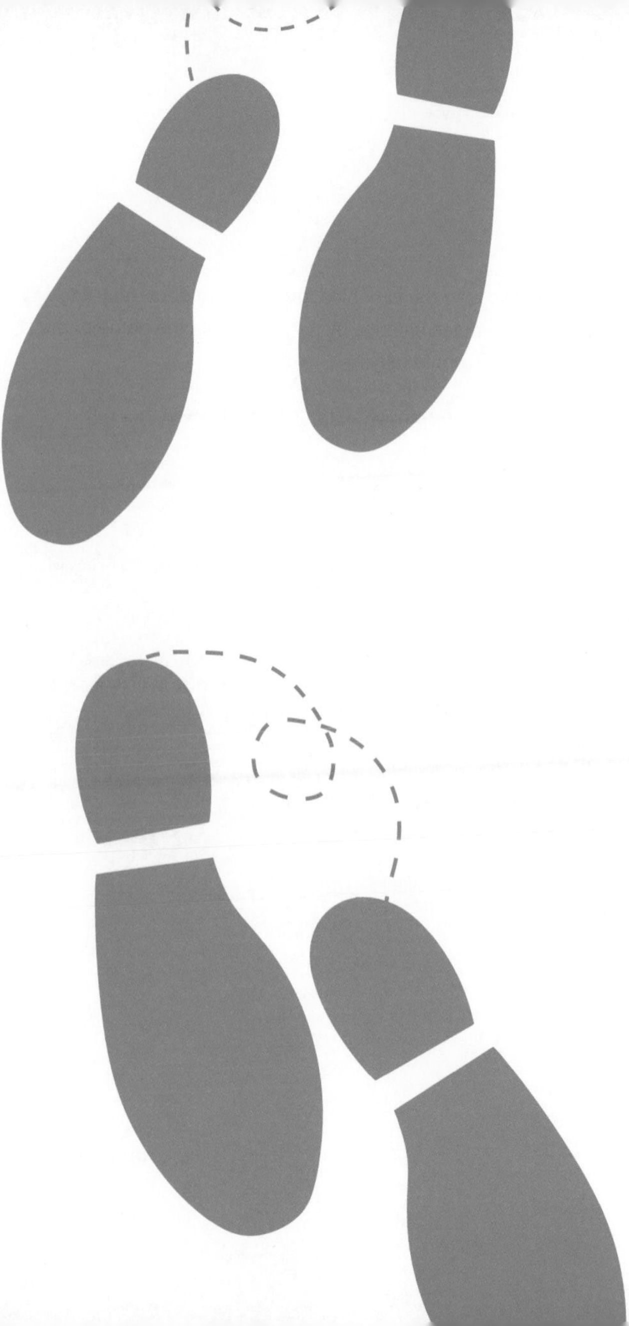

Descriptive statistics should accompany every statistical analysis. What measure of central tendency might be useful to report alongside this comparison?

....

Why would you run that measure of central tendency?

....

Answers

Descriptive statistics should accompany every statistical analysis. What measure of central tendency might be useful to report alongside this comparison?

Mean

....

Why would you run that measure of central tendency?

Because there are no outliers in the data.

....

35